Celebrations!

Ramadan and Id-ul-Fitr

Mandy Ross

Heinemann LIBRARY

H www.heinemann.co.uk/library
Visit our website to find out more information about Heinemann Library books.

To order:
☎ Phone 44 (0) 1865 888066
▤ Send a fax to 44 (0) 1865 314091
💻 Visit the Heinemann Bookshop at www.heinemann.co.uk/library to browse our catalogue and order online.

First published in Great Britain by Heinemann Library,
Halley Court, Jordan Hill, Oxford OX2 8EJ
a division of Reed Educational and Professional Publishing Ltd.
Heinemann is a registered trademark of Reed Educational & Professional Publishing Ltd.

OXFORD MELBOURNE AUCKLAND
JOHANNESBURG BLANTYRE GABORONE
IBADAN PORTSMOUTH (NH) USA CHICAGO

Designed by Celia Floyd
Originated by Ambassador Litho Ltd
Printed by Wing King Tong in Hong Kong

ISBN 0 431 13795 1 (hardback)　　　　ISBN 0 431 13803 6 (paperback)
06 05 04 03 02　　　　　　　　　　　06 05 04 03 02
10 9 8 7 6 5 4 3 2　　　　　　　　　 10 9 8 7 6 5 4 3 2 1

British Library Cataloguing in Publication Data

Ross, Mandy
　Ramadan and Id-ul-Fitr. – (Celebrations)
　1. Ramadan – Juvenile literature　2. Id ul-Fitr – Juvenile literature
　I. Title
　394.2'657

Acknowledgements

The Publishers would like to thank the following for permission to reproduce photographs:
Christine Osbourne: p21; Corbis: Earl & Nazima Kowall p5, David Turnley p11, Arthur Thevenart p18; Food Features: p6; Impact Photo: Robin Laurance p10; Peter Sanders: pp4, 16; Robert Harding Picture Library: Mohamed Amin p12; Trip: p8, H Rogers pp7, 14, 17, 19, 20, C Rennie p15

Cover photograph reproduced with permission of Trip: H Rogers

Our thanks to the Bradford Interfaith Education Centre for their comments in the preparation of this book.

Every effort has been made to contact copyright holders of any material reproduced in this book.
Any omissions will be rectified in subsequent printings if notice is given to the Publisher.

Contents

Words printed in **bold letters like these** are explained in the glossary.

Ramadan

Each day in the month of Ramadan, **Muslims** keep a strict fast. They eat no food and do not drink at all, in the hours of daylight. During these days, Muslims may say extra prayers, and go more often than usual to their place of **worship**, the **mosque** (also called a **masjid**).

At first, it is hard to fast. But as the days pass, Muslims say that they start to get used to living in this way. Ramadan is a special time when many Muslims feel close to God, whom they call **Allah**, and to their families.

This mosque is in Regent's Park, London. It has a dome and a tower, called a minaret.

The fast finishes at the end of the month, when the new moon has been seen in the sky. Then there are joyful celebrations and feasting for the festival of Id-ul-Fitr.

Ramadan was the month when Muslims believe that the **Qur'an**, their **holy** book, was revealed to the **prophet**, **Muhammad (pbuh)**. They believe that the Qur'an holds the word of Allah.

A page from the Qur'an, the Muslim holy book. It is written in Arabic, the language of Muhammad (pbuh).

The fast of Ramadan

During the month of Ramadan, most **Muslims** fast all day. They get up very early, before sunrise, to eat a small meal. Then they eat and drink nothing at all until sunset.

When the sun has set they may break their fast with a small snack. Then the family gathers to eat a proper meal.

Muslims believe that **fasting** shows obedience to **Allah**. They believe that it is good to feel hungry and yet to be able to wait to eat. Fasting also reminds Muslims that there are many people in the world who are hungry or thirsty.

It is traditional to break the fast each evening with fruit and nuts, before eating a meal.

Almost all Muslims keep the fast of Ramadan strictly. They believe that there will be a day of judgement when each person must explain the good and bad things they did in their life.

Not everyone has to fast, especially if it would cause them harm to do so. Young children do not have to fast, and nor do pregnant women, old people or those who are ill.

These Muslim children are sitting down with their family to eat their meal after sunset.

Muhammad (pbuh) and the Qur'an

Many **Muslims** celebrate the Night of Power on 27th day of Ramadan. This is the date they believe that the **Angel** Jibril (or Gabriel) gave the first part of the **Qur'an** to the prophet, **Muhammad (pbuh)**. They may spend time in the **mosque** or at home, reading the Qur'an.

Muhammad (pbuh) was born in about 570 CE in the city of **Makkah**, in the country we now call Saudi Arabia. Muhammad (pbuh) hated to see people **worshipping** gods made of clay, and fighting and cheating the poor. He went to the desert to think and pray.

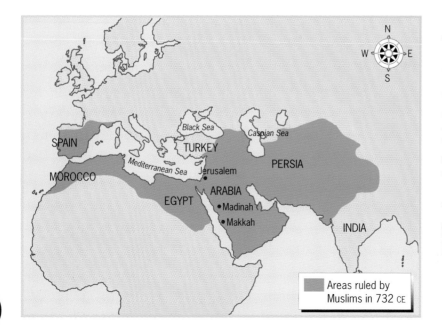

This map shows Makkah where Muhammad (pbuh) was born. Islam spread quickly, and by 732 CE, all of the area marked in green was under Muslim rule.

One night, alone in a desert cave, he saw the Angel Jibril, carrying a piece of cloth with writing on it. Although he had never learned to read or write, Muhammad (pbuh) found that he could read the words. These words were the first part of the Muslim holy book, the Qur'an. Later, the angel visited Muhammad (pbuh) again to tell him the rest of the Qur'an.

Muhammad (pbuh) started to teach people about Allah and the stories in the Qur'an. People began to follow his teachings, and **Islam** started to spread very quickly in the lands around Makkah and beyond. Today Islam is growing faster than any other **religion**.

The city of Makkah today.

Praying

Praying is the most important part of **Muslim worship**. Many Muslims pray five times every day. They always face in the direction of the holy city of **Makkah**. Muslims can go to the **mosque** to pray, but they can pray anywhere. 'All the world is a mosque,' said **Muhammad (pbuh)**.

Wudu

Before they pray, Muslims wash in a special way. This is called wudu. Wudu is not just about cleaning away dirt. Instead, it is to make a person fit to speak to **Allah**.

Praying at Badshahi Mosque in Pakistan.

At the mosque, men pray together in a big, open room. Women may pray in a different part of the room, in another room, or at home.

Muslim prayers follow a pattern, with movements including bowing, kneeling and touching the ground with your forehead. Different prayers are said in each position.

Muslims worship Allah and ask blessings for Muhammad (pbuh) and for Muslims everywhere. They may add their own

This Muslim man is kneeling on a beautiful prayer carpet to pray.

prayers at the end of the set prayers. When they have finished praying, they turn their head from side to side to salute other worshippers and the two invisible **angels** which they believe are always with each person.

The Five Pillars of Islam

A pillar is a strong column of stone or brick, which supports a building. The Five Pillars of Islam are not real, solid pillars. Instead they are the five most important things that **Muslims** believe in, which support the **religion** of **Islam**. Keeping the five pillars helps Muslims stay true to their religion.

Muslims on hajj, praying at the grand mosque at Makkah. Hajj is the fifth pillar of Islam.

These are the five pillars of Islam:

- The first pillar is faith. For Muslims, faith means believing that there is no God but **Allah**, and that **Muhammad (pbuh)** is the **prophet** of Allah.

- The second pillar is prayer. When it is time to pray, Muslims stop what they are doing and turn to face **Makkah**, whether or not they are at the **mosque**.

- The third pillar is giving **charity**, or money to people who are poor or needy.

- The fourth pillar is **fasting** at Ramadan. Muslims believe that fasting shows obedience to Allah.

- The fifth pillar is making a pilgrimage, or **holy** journey, to Makkah in Saudi Arabia. This is called hajj. Every Muslim hopes to go on hajj at least once.

Id-ul-Fitr

After a month of **fasting**, everyone is waiting for Id-ul-Fitr. But the festival cannot begin until the new moon has been seen in the sky.

In Britain, where the sky is often cloudy at night, **Muslim** leaders might telephone friends in hotter countries to ask whether the moon has been sighted there.

Once a new moon has been seen in the sky, Id-ul-Fitr can begin. This **mosque** is in Dubai.

When the moon appears, the celebrations can begin. People gather at the mosque for special prayers, and then there are celebrations at home.

Zakat-ul-Fitr

An important part of the celebrations is to give money to **charity**. Charities give money or food to poor people to make sure that everyone can take part in the feasting for Id-ul-Fitr. Giving money for charity is also one of the five pillars of Islam.

A collection box for Zakat-ul-Fitr or charity at Id.

Celebrating Id-ul-Fitr

Id-ul-Fitr is a happy time. After praying at the **mosque**, **Muslims** go visiting friends and relations. They may bring gifts, such as sugared almonds and other sweets, beautifully wrapped in boxes with ribbons. Children are often given money at Id-ul-Fitr.

Dressed in their best clothes, these children are visiting relatives.

Everyone wears their best clothes, and they may have new outfits for the occasion. There are parties and special meals, and sometimes people stay up all night to celebrate.

At Id-ul-Fitr and other celebrations, many women and girls paint patterns on their hands using henna, a kind of dye. This is called mehndi.

Intricate mehndi patterns like this can take hours to complete.

Islamic art and calligraphy

At Id-ul-Fitr, many people send greetings cards decorated with Islamic art and **calligraphy**. Islamic art never shows pictures of people or animals, because **Muslims** believe it is wrong for an artist to try to copy **Allah** by making even an image of a living thing.

Mosques are often beautifully decorated with paintings or carvings of flowers and leaves, or intricate patterns made with coloured tiles. Words in Arabic from the **Qur'an** may be carved in beautiful flowing shapes.

Decorative tiles at Selemiye Mosque in Turkey. The calligraphy at the top shows words in Arabic.

How to make an Id card

You will need a piece of card or stiff
paper and coloured pens or pencils.

1. Fold the card. Keep the fold on the right
   hand side.
2. Design and colour a picture or pattern on
   the front, using flowers and leaves, or the
   moon and stars, or showing a mosque.
3. Inside on the left hand side, you can write
   'Id Mubarak', which means Happy Id.

These girls are looking at some home-made
paintings and greetings cards for Id-ul-Fitr.

Around the world

In countries where most people are **Muslim**, restaurants stay closed every day during Ramadan. Nobody eats food during the day. But they may need to go shopping to buy food to cook for the evening meal at the end of the day's fast.

This restaurant in Tunisia is closed for Id.

Id-ul-Fitr is a national holiday in Muslim countries such as Pakistan or Algeria. Nobody has to go to school or work for a day or two. Everybody goes visiting relatives and friends. There may be fairs, parades and entertainments. Families may go for a walk together in the park to see the celebrations.

Id is a good time for special day trips and family outings. Children look forward to these treats at the end of Ramadan.

Families walking in the park in Cairo at Id-ul-Fitr.

The Muslim calendar

The **Muslim** calendar is a lunar calendar, which means that it is based on the moon. There are 12 lunar months, each with 29 or 30 days.

The lunar year is about 11 days shorter than the western calendar year from January to December. So each year, Muslim festivals fall on an earlier date according to the western calendar.

In some years, Ramadan falls in the summertime when the days are long. But when it comes in the winter, the shorter days make fasting much easier.

The Muslim calendar started in the year 622 **CE**. This was the year that **Muhammad (pbuh)** journeyed to the city of Madinah, and many more people started to follow his teachings. The year 2001 CE is the year 1421 and 1422 in the Muslim calendar.

Glossary

Allah the Muslim name for God

angel Muslims believe that an angel is a spirit or being that works for Allah

calligraphy artistic handwriting

CE stands for the Common Era. People of all religions can use this, rather than the Christian AD, which counts from the birth of Jesus Christ. The year numbers are not changed.

charity giving money or help to people who need it

fasting to go without food and drink

holy respected because it is to do with God

Islam the religion followed by Muslims

Makkah the city where Muhammad (pbuh) was born. Makkah is in the country we now call Saudi Arabia, in the Middle East.

masjid the Muslim place of worship (also called mosque)

mosque the Muslim place of worship (also called masjid)

Muhammad (pbuh) the man Muslims believe was the last prophet

Muslim someone who follows the religion of Islam

pbuh stands for 'peace be upon him'. Muslims always say or write this after they use Muhammad's name, or the name of other prophets.

prophet someone who tells people what God wants

Qur'an the Muslim holy book

religion belief in God or gods

worship show respect and love for God

Index